THE NEW
CROSS STITCH

THE NEW
CROSS STITCH

A COLLECTION OF INSPIRATIONAL DESIGNS

DOROTHY WOOD

Photographs by Lucy Mason

HERMES
HOUSE

This edition first published in 1997 by Hermes House

© Anness Publishing Limited 1997

Hermes House is an imprint of
Anness Publishing
Limited
Hermes House
88-89 Blackfriars Road
London
SE1 8HA

This edition distributed in Canada by
Raincoast Books
8680 Cambie Street
Vancouver
British Columbia V6P 6M9

ISBN 1901289 84 2

A CIP catalogue record for this book
is available from the British Library.

Publisher: Joanna Lorenz
Project Editor: Joanne Rippin
Designer: Janet James
Photographer: Lucy Mason
Charts: Ethan Danielson

Printed and bound in Hong Kong

1 3 5 7 9 10 8 6 4 2

CONTENTS

THREADS

Although stranded cotton is probably the most popular and versatile thread for cross stitch embroidery, there is an amazing range of different threads available.

Coton perlé produces attractive raised stitches and tapestry wool makes big, chunky cross stitches on a seven or eight count canvas. Some of the projects in this book use other familiar threads such as coton à broder or soft cotton but many are worked in new threads such as silky Marlitt or the more rustic flower thread which is ideal for stitching on linen. New threads are appearing on the market all the time. Look out for unusual flower threads which have been dyed in shaded natural colours and metallic threads which have been specially made for cross stitching.

TAPESTRY WOOL

Although traditionally associated with needlepoint, tapestry wool is also suitable for some cross stitch. It is usually worked on a chunky seven count canvas and makes a warm, hard-wearing cover for cushions, stools and chairs.

FLOWER THREAD OR NORDIN

This rustic cotton thread is ideal for working on evenweave linen fabrics. In thickness it is equivalent to two or three strands of stranded cotton. It is available in solid colours, but look out for the space-dyed skeins.

MARLITT

A lustrous rayon thread, Marlitt has been introduced to provide the sheen and beauty of silk at an economical price. Although only available in solid colours, it has four strands, allowing the colours to be mixed "in the needle".

STRANDED COTTON

This is the most popular embroidery thread and is available in over 400 different colours. It is a versatile thread which can be divided into six separate strands. The separated strands of several colours can be intermingled to create a mottled effect when stitched.

COTON PERLÉ

This twisted thread has a distinct pearly sheen and is available in over 300 different colours. It comes in several different thicknesses and is generally used to produce a slightly raised effect on a variety of fabrics.

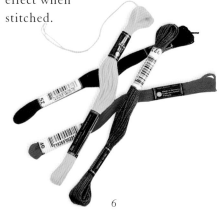

METALLIC THREADS

Although traditionally unsuitable for cross stitch embroidery, some metallic threads are now specially made to sew through fabric. They are available in a range of colours as well as gold and silver. Finer metallic threads known as blending filaments can be worked together with strands of embroidery thread to add an attractive sparkle or sheen.

FABRICS

Evenweave fabrics have the same number of threads running in each direction. The number of threads in each 2½ cm (1 in) of fabric determines the gauge or "count". The larger the number of threads, the finer the fabric. Aida and Hardanger are woven and measured in blocks of threads. However, cross stitches worked on 28 count linen are the same size as those on 14 count Aida because the stitches are worked over two threads of linen.

LINEN

Traditionally pure linen was used, but there are now several different mixed fibre evenweave fabrics in a wide range of colours.

AIDA AND HARDANGER

These popular fabrics have groups of threads woven together to produce distinctive blocks over which the embroidery is worked.

Aida comes in 8–18 count whereas Hardanger is a 22 count fabric. It can be used for fine stitching or worked as an 11 count fabric.

EVENWEAVE BANDS

Aida or evenweave bands come in a variety of widths. Some are plain and others have decorative edges. Once stitched, these bands can be applied to a background fabric or made up into bows, tie-backs or bags.

FANCY WEAVES

Fabrics specially woven with distinct areas for cross stitching are suitable for making into napkins, tablecloths and cot covers. There are also some unusual evenweaves which have linen or Lurex threads interwoven into the fabric for special effects.

CANVAS

Double and single thread canvas is usually associated with needlepoint but can be used successfully for cross stitch embroidery. Wool and coton perlé are particularly suitable threads for using when stitching on canvas.

WASTE CANVAS

A non-interlocked canvas is used to work cross stitch on non-evenweave fabric or ready-made items. It is specially made so that it can be frayed and removed after the cross stitch is worked.

NON-FRAY FABRICS

Plastic canvas, vinyl weave and stitching paper are all used for cross stitch projects where it is important that the fabric should not fray.

ADDITIONAL FABRICS

Iron-on interfacing is sometimes used to provide a backing for the cross stitch design.

Fusible bonding web is generally used for appliqué.

1: linens; 2: plastic canvas, stitching paper, fusible bonding web, iron-on interfacing; 3: aida and linen bands; 4: 14 and 10 count waste canvas; 5: aida and white Hardanger; 6: canvases; 7: fancy weaves.

TECHNIQUES:BEGINNING

PREPARING THE FABRIC

Many of the projects in this book use evenweave fabrics which tend to fray easily, therefore it is advisable to finish the edges before starting the embroidery. An allowance has been made for neatening the edges in calculating the materials needed.

MASKING TAPE

A quick method for projects worked on inter-locking bar frames. The tape can be stapled or pinned to a frame.

ZIGZAG

Machine-stitched zigzag is used when embroidering parts of a garment since the seams will be neatened ready to stitch together.

BLANKET STITCH

This is the best all round method of neatening evenweave fabric. Either turn a small hem or stitch round the raw edge.

LEFT TO RIGHT: masking tape, zigzag and blanket stitch.

COVERING A HOOP

Embroidery hoops (frames) have two rings, one is solid and the other has a screw-fastening. The fabric is sandwiched between the two rings and the screw-fastening adjusted to keep the fabric taut. In order to protect the fabric and stitches from damage, the inner ring is wrapped with narrow cotton tape. Remember that some delicate fabrics can be damaged in an embroidery hoop (frame). In these cases it is advisable to use a large hoop which extends beyond the cross stitch area. Interlocking bar frames are ideal for small projects and a rotating frame is best for large pieces of work.

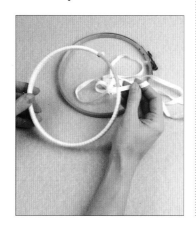

STARTING & FINISHING THREADS

There are several ways to begin a piece of cross stitch. Finish by sliding the needle under several stitches and trimming the end.

1 Fold a length of cotton in half and thread into the needle. Work the first half of the cross stitch, then thread the needle through the loop on the reverse side.

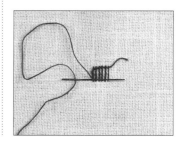

2 Leave a length of 5 cm (2 in) thread at the back of the fabric and weave this in when you have worked a block of stitches.

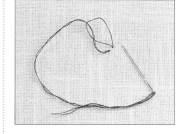

WASTE CANVAS

This technique allows charted cross stitch to be worked on non-evenweave fabric or ready-made items such as towels and cushions. Waste canvas is specially made so that the threads can be easily removed. It is only available in 10 and 14 count but you could use ordinary canvas provided that the threads are not interlocked.

1 Tack (baste) a piece of canvas onto the area to be stitched. Make sure there will be plenty of canvas round the design once it is complete.

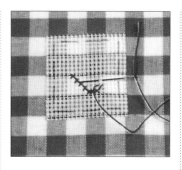

2 Work the cross stitch design over the canvas and through the fabric. Take care to make all the stitches as even as you possibly can.

3 Once complete, fray the canvas and pull the threads out one at a time. It will be easier if you tug the canvas gently to loosen the threads.

TECHNIQUES:FINISHING

MITRED CORNER

Tablecloths and mats can be finished neatly with mitred corners. These reduce bulk and make a secure hem which can be laundered safely.

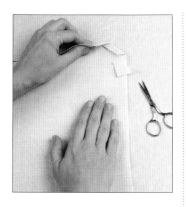 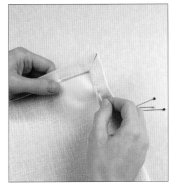

1 Fold the hem, run your fingers along and open out. Cut across the corner from crease to crease and refold the hem.

2 Turn under a further 0.5 cm (¼ in) and pin the hem in place. Slip stitch the mitred corner and machine or hand stitch the hem.

STRETCHING

As a general rule embroidery should always be stretched using thread so that it can be easily removed and cleaned in the future. However, small projects which may be kept for only a limited time can be quickly and successfully mounted using double-sided tape.

1 Cut the card (cardboard) to the required size and stick double-sided tape along all the edges. Trim across the corners and remove the paper backing. Stretch the fabric onto the tape and mitre the corners neatly.

MOUNTING

If a project such as a sampler or picture is likely to be kept for a long time, great care should be taken in mounting the finished work. Acid-free mount board (backing board) or paper should be used under the embroidery and glue or tape which leave an acid residue on the fabric should be avoided.

The following easy method of mounting ensures that the embroidery will be absolutely straight and exactly where you want it.

1 Cut the mount board to size and mark the mid point across the top and bottom of the board. Allow for a wider border at the bottom if required. Mark the mid point of the embroidery at each side of the board and draw in the lines. Lay the embroidery face down on a flat surface and place the mount board on top of it.

2 Line up the guidelines on the embroidery with the lines on the board. Fold the top edge over and put a pin into the mount board at the centre line. Stretch the fabric slightly and put another pin at the bottom. Repeat the process at the sides. Work your way along each edge from the centre out putting in pins every 2.5 cm (1 in) keeping the grain of the fabric straight.

3 Using a long length of double thread, sew from side to side spacing the stitches about 12 mm (½ in) apart. Join in more thread using an overhand knot. Once complete lift the threads up one at a time to pull them tight and secure. Mitre or fold the corners and repeat along the remaining sides.

TRACING & TRANSFERRING

Nowadays, with the right computer equipment, it is possible to scan pictures directly into a cross stitch or graphics program and produce your own charts. The design can be simplified on screen by merging colours to reduce the number of different colours needed. Colours can be changed readily and interesting details, borders or motifs can be copied and used to create new attractive designs.

Most of us though, still need to transfer a design onto graph paper to create a chart for cross stitch. You can draw directly onto graph paper, but the finished design can look "boxy". It is possible to trace and transfer a simple motif but the simplest method is to use an "Easy grid." This is a sheet of clear acetate which has been printed with grid lines. The grids come in different sizes to match the various counts of fabric. You can also use a colour photocopier to enlarge or reduce the design before using the correct count grid to make the chart.

1 Choose a picture which is the same size as the finished cross stitch. Lay the selected grid on top of the picture and tape down. Either work the cross stitch directly from the grid or transfer the design onto graph paper. If a square is mainly one colour then stitch it that colour. If the square is half and half, work two three-quarter cross stitches, one in each colour to fill the square.

NEEDLEWORK TIP

If the picture you want to use is larger or smaller than the proposed size of cross stitch, you can use a different count Easy grid to scale the chart up or down. For example, you might want a 40 cm (16 in) square cross stitch design for a cushion using tapestry wool on 7 count canvas, but the picture you have is only 20 cm (8 in) square. In this case use a 14 count Easy grid to make a chart from the picture and the design will work out the correct size.

TO TRACE THE DESIGN

If the picture you wish to use is much smaller than the finished size of the proposed cross stitch, it is often quicker to trace and enlarge the design using squared paper. Remember that the final result you achieve will depend upon how accurately you trace the initial picture. When tracing, always use a very sharp hard pencil and take care to draw the details exactly.

1 Lay the tracing paper over the picture area and secure with masking tape. Draw round the edges of the design motif carefully with a sharp pencil. Try to include as many of the tiny details as possible to make the enlarged design more accurate and interesting.

2 Turn the tracing paper over onto the graph paper and position the design . Draw along the lines carefully. In this way the design will be inverted. To reproduce the original motif, scribble over the reverse side of the tracing and then draw over the lines.

TO ENLARGE THE DESIGN

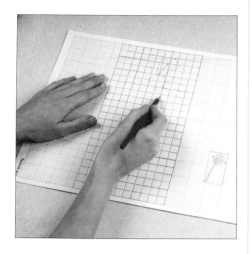

1 Draw a line round the design area and adapt the motif to suit. In this case, a stem has been added to the flower head.

Draw a similarly shaped large rectangle the exact size of the proposed cross stitch design. Count the squares across and down the side of the small motif and then mark out the same number on the larger grid. Working from left to right, square by square transfer the lines from the small to the larger grid.

2 Refer to the original picture and mark the shaded areas on the petals and flower centre. Use pens or pencils to colour the design. The design can be worked directly from the graph paper using 10 count waste canvas or use the appropriate sheet of Easy grid to stitch on other counts of evenweave fabric.

Above: Once you have transferred a design you can use it as a small detail, or a large, bold, single motif, as on this cushion.

TO ROTATE THE DESIGN

At this stage, the design could be transferred onto computer. There are many cross stitch design packages now available which allow you greater flexibility and speed when trying out different colourways of the same design. Cross stitch computer programs also enable you to flip motifs vertically and horizontally as well as rotating them through 45 or 90 degrees. This feature is invaluable when designing borders and turning corners. If you do not have access to a computer the traditional method of rotating, using a mirror is quite satisfactory.

1 Stand a mirror tile upright on the cross stitch chart at an angle of 45 degrees. On a separate piece of graph paper draw out the corner design you can see reflected in the mirror. To get a mirror image, hold the mirror straight along the edge of the cross stitch motif and draw the reversed image.

CUSHION

This chunky cup design is ideal for conservatory or kitchen chair cushions.

YOU WILL NEED

30 x 46 cm (12 x 18 in) 7 count Sudan canvas

tacking (basting) thread

needle

rotating frame

tapestry wool Anchor 8006, 8116, 8306, 8528, 8626, 8986

tapestry needle

pins

1.5 m (1½ yd) cream piping

sewing machine

sewing thread

30 x 46 cm (12 x 18 in) cream backing fabric

scissors

25 x 38 cm (10 x 15 in) cushion pad

WORKING THE CROSS STITCH

Tack (baste) a guideline in both directions across the middle of the canvas. Begin in the centre, working a cup above and below the horizontal guideline. Work the cups on either side, reversing the position of the spots and stripes. Repeat the wine and green lines round the design if you wish.

1 To make up: block the design when complete. Pin and tack the piping round the edge of the cross stitch, over-lapping the ends along the bottom. Stitch close to the piping along that edge.

2 With the embroidery to the inside, pin and tack the backing in place. Stitch round the remaining three sides. Trim the seams and corners and turn through. Insert the cushion pad and slip stitch the opening to complete the project.

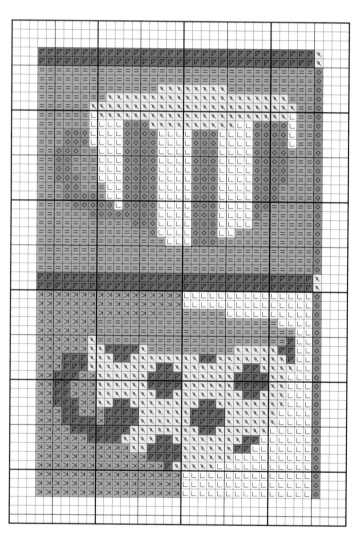

Anchor tapestry wool		
= = 8306	◇ ◇	8986
L L 8006	⊼ ⊼	8116
▷ ⊿ 8626	▷ ▷	8528

EMBROIDERED DUNGAREES AND HAT BAND

YOU WILL NEED

*denim dungarees with
a plain bib*

*10 x 15 cm (4 x 6 in) 14 count
waste canvas*

pins

tacking (basting) thread

needle

pencil

*stranded cotton Anchor 6, 9, 46,
238, 291, 896*

embroidery needle

straw hat

*60 cm (24 in) of 2.5 cm (1 in)
wide cream Aida band,
Zweigart E7002*

scissors

sewing thread

*These projects match perfectly and make a lovely design for a child's
dungarees and straw hat.*

TO MAKE THE DUNGAREES

WORKING THE CROSS STITCH

The design area for this pig measures 7 x 13 cm (2¾ x 5 in) and is suitable to stitch on age 5–6 dungarees. If you want to embroider a larger area, use 10 count canvas which gives a design size of 10 x 18 cm (4 x 7 in).

Pin and tack (baste) the waste canvas in the middle of the bib. Mark the centre of the canvas with a pencil and work the cross stitch using two strands of cotton (three for 10 count). Once complete, remove the canvas threads one at a time and then press.

Anchor			Backstitch
- - 6	2 2	291	—— 896
1 1 9	3 3	46	
1 1 896	4 4	238	☆ Middle point

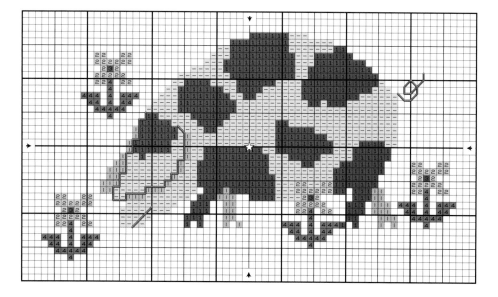

TO MAKE THE HAT BAND

WORKING THE CROSS STITCH

Measure the hat and cut the Aida band 5 cm (2 in) longer. Fold the band in half and put in a pin to mark the centre. Work a flower on the centre line and continue the design out towards each end. Try to finish with a flower or the border pattern.

1 To make up: fit the band round the hat. Turn one end in and pin on top of the other end. Slip stitch the ends together. If necessary, secure the band onto the hat by stitching it with prick stitch (tiny running stitches on the front and long stitches on the back).

Anchor	
2 2	291
3 3	46
4 4	238

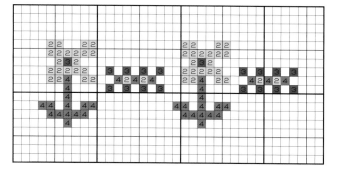

EMBROIDERED BOOK

This little book is made from off-cuts of card (cardboard) and fabrics and contains some small sheets of handmade paper.

YOU WILL NEED

11 x 13 cm (4⅜ x 5 in) gingham

stranded cotton Anchor 352, 890

embroidery needle

25 cm (10 in) square of blue moleskin or denim

scissors

15 cm (6 in) square of floral cotton fabric

15 cm (6 in) square of brown cotton fabric

15 x 30 cm (6 x 12 in) fusible bonding web

all-purpose glue

two pieces of 15 x 18 cm (6 x 7 in) card (cardboard)

masking tape

23 x 38 cm (9 x 15 in) striped cotton

double-sided tape

18 x 33 cm (7 x 13 in) check cotton

pinking shears

5 sheets of hand-made paper 18 x 33 cm (7 x 13 in)

WORKING THE CROSS STITCH

Cross stitch a border round the edge of the piece of gingham. Cut a piece of moleskin to fit inside the border and sew onto the gingham with larger, cruder cross stitches. Iron the fusible bonding web onto the reverse sides of the brown and floral cotton fabrics. Cut out the tree shape and eight petal templates. Remove the backing paper and iron the pieces in place on the moleskin. Sew tiny cross stitches round the shapes. Stitch three crosses along the bottom of the tree and one in the centre of each flower and press on the reverse side. Cut a 12 x 14 cm (4¾ x 5½ in) piece of moleskin and stick to the back of the embroidered gingham with bonding web or glue.

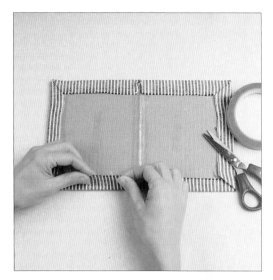

1 To make up: tape the two pieces of card together leaving a 1 cm (⅜ in) gap so that they will fold up like a book. Lay the card in the middle of the reverse side of the striped cotton. Put double-sided tape along the outside edges of the card and stretch the fabric onto the tape, mitring the corners neatly.

2 Cut round the edges of the check fabric with pinking shears to fit onto the inside cover and stick in place. Fold the paper in half crossways and position in the middle of the book. Stitch the pages into the book down the centre fold. Stick the embroidered panel onto the front of the cover to finish.

DECORATIVE MIRROR

This small mirror is just the right size to fit into a handbag and special enough to take with you for an evening out.

YOU WILL NEED

two 15 cm (6 in) squares of 27 count Linda, Zweigart E1235

tacking (basting) thread

needle

small embroidery frame (flexihoop)

fine gold braid Kreinik 002

Anchor Marlitt 845, 870, 1034, 1040, 1140

tapestry needle

craft knife

safety ruler

11 cm (4⅜ in) square of mount board (backing board)

double-sided tape

11 cm (4⅜ in) (approximately) square mirror

scissors

sewing thread

WORKING THE CROSS STITCH

Tack (baste) guidelines across the middle of the linen in both directions. Work the outlines in gold braid over two threads, then complete the mirror's motifs and border using two strands of Marlitt.

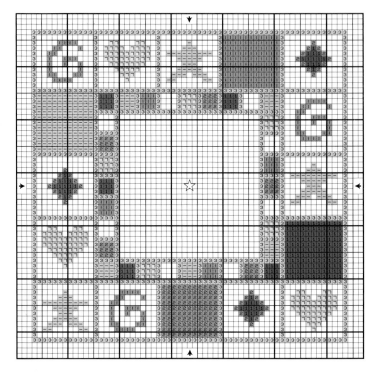

Anchor Marlitt		
⊓⊓ 1034	ɜɜ	Kreinik fine gold braid 002
– – 845		
I I 870		
▪ ▪ 1040	☆	Middle point
2 2 1140		

1 To make up: press carefully on the reverse side, as Marlitt is a synthetic thread. Measure the outside edge of the embroidery, then trim the mount board (backing board) and cut the mirror to size using a glass cutter, or ask a glazier to do it for you. Measure the middle panel and cut the centre out of the mount board.

2 Lay the embroidered linen right side down and cut into the corners of the middle panel. Place the mount board on top and put double-sided tape round the inside edge. Stretch the fabric onto the tape and then lay the mirror on top, face down.

3 Trim the excess fabric to 2.5 cm (1 in) and put more tape round the edge of the mirror. Stretch the fabric onto the mirror back, mitring the corners neatly. Trim the second piece of linen, fold under a small hem and oversew onto the back of the mirror to finish.

GREETINGS CARD

*Greetings cards often have a very short life, but this card comes
ready mounted and could be displayed in a small frame.*

WORKING
THE CROSS STITCH

Stretch the linen in a
small embroidery frame
(flexihoop). Work the
cross stitch over two
threads in the middle of
the linen. Work the stars
in backstitch over four
threads and then press
the linen on the reverse
side when complete.

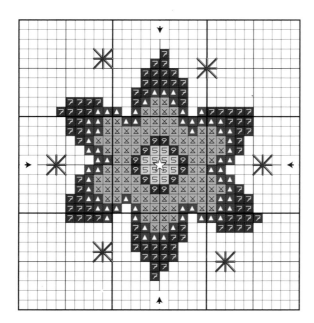

YOU WILL NEED

*15 cm (6 in) square of white 28
count Irish linen*

*small embroidery frame
(flexihoop)*

*Anchor Nordin 119, 127, 134,
144, 290*

tapestry needle

*10 x 15 cm (4 x 6 in)
mount board (backing board)*

craft knife

safety ruler

double-sided tape

*two different oddments of blue
gingham*

scissors

	Anchor Nordin
5 5	290
7 7	134
9 9	127
X X	144
▲ ▲	119
	Backstitch
—	127
☆	Middle point

1 To make up: cut a
10 cm (4 in) square
from the mount board
(backing board). Score a
line across the remaining
strip of board 2.5 cm (1 in)
from one end. Stick this
end of the strip onto the
back of the square to make
a simple stand.

2 Cut one piece of
gingham slightly
smaller than the mount
board and stick just above
the middle. Repeat with
the second gingham then
trim the embroidery and
stick in place.

TABLE MAT

*The colours of the fabric and thread in this geometric design could
easily be adapted to suit any room setting.*

YOU WILL NEED

*30 x 40 cm (12 x 16 in)
terracotta 28 count evenweave*

tacking (basting) thread

needle

embroidery hoop (frame)

*stranded cotton DMC 310, 743,
712, 3053*

tapestry needle

pins

sewing thread

scissors

WORKING THE CROSS STITCH

Tack (baste) guidelines across the
middle of the linen in both directions
and work the shapes in cross stitch
using two strands of cotton over two
threads of linen. Count the threads
carefully between the shapes.

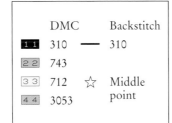

	DMC	Backstitch
1 1	310	—— 310
2 2	743	
3 3	712	☆ Middle
4 4	3053	point

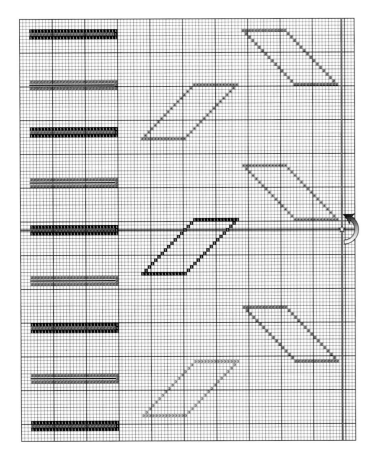

1 To make up: leaving a 5 cm
(2 in) tail of threads from each
of the side stripes, work the cross
stitch and then the backstitch.

2 Press on the reverse side and
turn under a small hem down
both long sides of the mat. Pin and
slip stitch in position.

3 Using the ends of the loose
threads as guidelines, fold over
a deeper hem at each end. Pin and
slip stitch to complete. Press the
mat on the reverse side and trim the
fringes to 3 cm (1¼ in).

PHOTOFRAME

This frame was inspired by the Art Deco period at the beginning of the twentieth century which brought about the first "modern" designs.

WORKING THE CROSS STITCH

Start in one corner of the linen about 4 cm (1½ in) in from the sides. Work the cross stitch in rows across or down for a smooth finish, using two strands of cotton. Press the embroidery on the reverse side when complete.

YOU WILL NEED

25 x 30 cm (10 x 12 in) white 14 count Aida

stranded cotton Anchor 259, 273, 308, 311, 870, 872, 968, 9159

tapestry needle

18 x 23 cm (7 x 9 in) mount board (backing board)

craft knife

safety ruler

double-sided tape

scissors

76 cm (30 in) of 2.5 cm (1 in) wood strip

hand saw

sandpaper

all-purpose glue

staple gun

masking tape

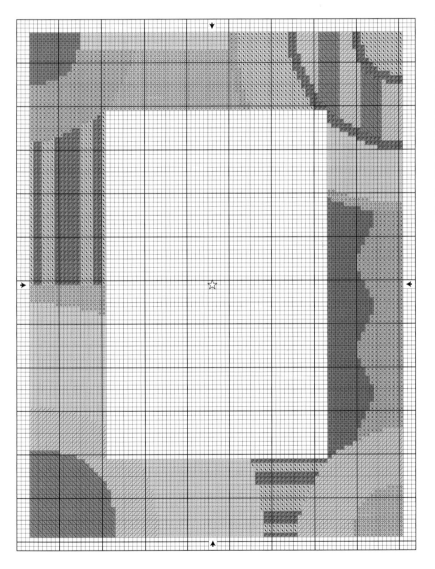

	Anchor
▨▨	308
⁚⁚⁚	259
⇥⇥	9159
◇◇	870
↘↘	311
◪◪	872
⁄⁄	968
◺◺	273
☆	Middle point

1 To make up: measure the embroidery, cut a mount exactly the same size and put double-sided tape round the inside edge. Cut into the inner corners of the embroidery and lay the mount on top. Trim the excess fabric and stretch on the tape.

2 Saw two strips of wood to fit lengthways on the back of the mount and two shorter strips to fit in between. Sand the ends and glue in position at the edge of the mount. Insert some staples across the joins for extra strength.

3 Mitre the corners and stretch the fabric onto the back of the frame. Use staples to hold in position and trim away the excess fabric. Cover the raw edges with masking tape. Make a cord using one of the embroidery threads and stick round the front edge of the frame to finish.

TIEBACKS

These big sunflowers stand out beautifully against the dark blue and white gingham fabric.

YOU WILL NEED

1 m (1 yd) of 90 cm (36 in) wide blue and white gingham

scissors

18 x 50 cm (7 x 20 in) 14 count waste canvas

pins

tacking (basting) thread

needle

stranded cotton DMC 300, 301, 400, 433, 742, 743, 904, 906, 938, 977, 986

embroidery needle

tracing paper

pencil

36 x 66 cm (14 x 26 in) medium weight iron-on interfacing

sewing machine

sewing thread

four white "D" rings

WORKING THE CROSS STITCH

If you can buy evenweave gingham, which is produced but is not readily available, work the design directly onto the fabric. Cut the gingham into four 23 x 68 cm (9 x 27 in) pieces. Fold one piece in four to find the centre and open out. Pin and tack (baste) half the waste canvas in the centre of the right hand side. Mark the centre of the waste canvas and work the cross stitch using two strands of cotton. Once complete, remove the canvas one thread at a time and press the embroidery on the reverse side.

DMC					
==	300	⋈⋈	742	ии	938
⋮⋮	301	▽▽	743	∧∧	977
>>	400	//	904	⋉⋉	986
◇◇	433	\\	906	☆	Middle point

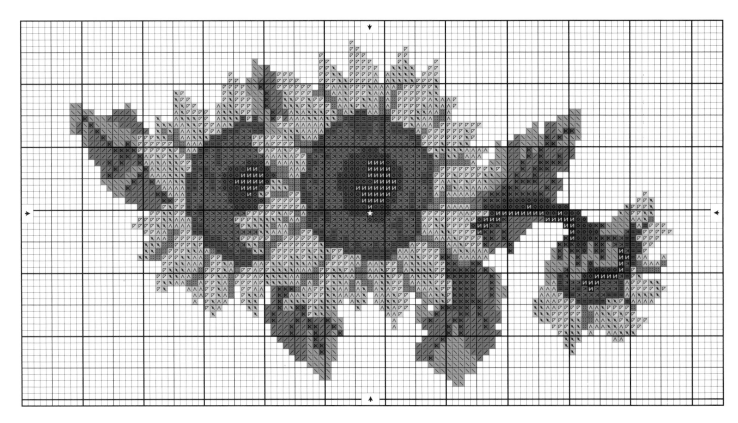

1 To make up: trace and enlarge the template onto tracing paper. Cut out a back and front from the tieback pattern, making sure that the sunflower is positioned correctly. Iron interfacing to the back pattern piece. With right sides together, sew the front and back together along both long sides. Trim the seams and snip into the curves.

2 Turn the tieback through, roll the edges between your thumb and first finger to centre the seams and press on the reverse side. Turn each end over the straight edge of a "D" ring, folding the excess fabric into tucks. Turn under a small hem and stitch securely. Make a second tieback in exactly the same way, stitching a mirror image of the sunflower on the left hand side of the gingham.

TOWEL

This towel is designed to match the sunflower tiebacks.
They would make a co-ordinating set for a plain white bathroom.

YOU WILL NEED

navy blue towel

25 cm (10 in) square of 14
count waste canvas

pins

tacking (basting) thread

needle

stranded cotton DMC 300, 301,
400, 433, 742, 743, 938, 977

embroidery needle

scissors

WORKING THE CROSS STITCH

Pin and tack (baste) the canvas at one
end of the towel where you wish to
stitch the motif. Work the cross stitch
over two pairs of threads using six
strands of cotton. You will get a better
result if the strands are separated and
recombined before stitching. Once
complete, fray and remove the canvas
threads one at a time. Press lightly
with a steam iron on the reverse side,
taking care not to damage the towel.

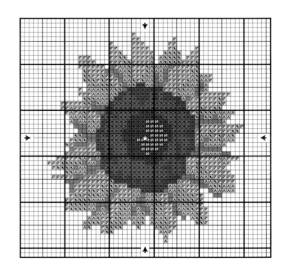

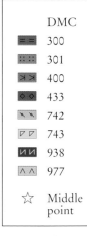

	DMC
==	300
⋮⋮	301
►►	400
◇◇	433
↖↖	742
▽▽	743
ИИ	938
∧∧	977
☆	Middle point

DAISY CUSHION

The petal colour on this huge daisy could be changed to match a different check cushion. Choose a dark and light shade of the same colour.

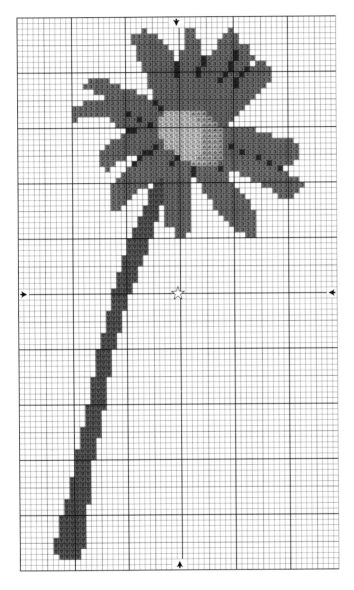

WORKING
THE CROSS STITCH

Pin and tack (baste) the waste canvas in the middle of the cushion cover with the opening to the bottom. Fit a large embroidery hoop (frame) on the front of the cushion cover. Mark the centre of the canvas and work the cross stitch using three strands of cotton.

YOU WILL NEED

30 cm (12 in) check cushion cover

15 x 30 cm (6 x 12 in) 10 count waste canvas

pins

tacking (basting) thread

needle

large embroidery hoop (frame)

pencil

stranded cotton Anchor 45, 212, 305, 306, 891, 896

embroidery needle

30 cm (12 in) cushion pad

Anchor	
2 2	45
3 3	896
4 4	306
5 5	305
6 6	891
▽ ▽	212

1 To make up: once the cover is complete, fray and remove the canvas threads one at a time. Press the embroidery on the reverse side, then turn the cover through and insert the cushion pad to finish.

GARDEN APRON

This big apron, with its large pocket, is ideal for holding small tools and protecting your clothes while working in the garden.

YOU WILL NEED

paper

pencil

90 cm (1 yd) of 115 cm (45 in) wide sand canvas

tailor's chalk

scissors

pins

sewing machine

sewing thread

tacking (basting) thread

needle

safety pin

20 cm (8 in) square of 10 count waste canvas

stranded cotton Anchor 46, 212, 226, 238, 316, 926

embroidery needle

WORKING THE CROSS STITCH

You may find it easier to work the cross stitch after you have made up the apron. Pin and tack (baste) the waste canvas in the middle of the bib. Work the cross stitch and the backstitch details on the plants using three strands of cotton. Then stitch the French knots. Remove the waste canvas before working the rest of the backstitch. Mark the position of the squares and stitch along the grain of the canvas to complete the design.

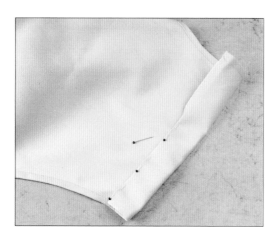

1 To make up: enlarge the pattern pieces and draw round them onto the canvas. Cut out two pockets, one front pattern piece and three 5 x 50 cm (2 x 20 in) strips. Turn over and stitch a small hem along the curved edges, the sides and bottom of the apron. Fold over 12 mm (½ in) along the top edge and then a further 2.5 cm (1 in). Pin, tack (baste) and stitch round all sides of the turning.

2 Fold the strips in half lengthways. Sew 12 mm (½ in) from the raw edge, leaving the straps open at one end, and turn through with a safety pin. Tuck the raw edges inside and press the straps. Pin and tack one strap to either side of the apron and the other one to the top of the bib. Machine stitch in a rectangle to secure the straps. Stitch again for extra strength.

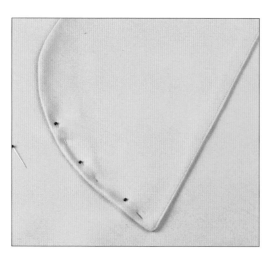

3 Sew the pocket pieces together, with right sides facing, leaving an 8 cm (3 in) gap along the straight edge. Trim and snip the curves, then turn through. Roll the edges between your fingers to make a good curved edge and press. Top stitch the straight edge, pin and tack to the apron and stitch in place. Stitch round the curved edge again for extra strength and sew straight down the centre of the pocket in the same way. Once complete, pin and tack the waste canvas in the middle of the bib.

Anchor	Backstitch	
3 3 926	——— 238	☆ Middle point
4 4 316	——— 212	
▽ ▽ 212	French knots	
↑ ↑ 226	🌑 46	

NOAH'S ARK

Noah's Ark is a perennial favourite and this design with its colourful animals and bright border is particularly appealing.

YOU WILL NEED

30 x 36 cm (12 x 14 in) white 22 count Hardanger

tacking (basting) thread

needle

interlocking bar frame

stranded cotton DMC white, 310, 444, 666, 702, 797, 970, 996

tapestry needle

25 x 30 cm (10 x 12 in) mount board (backing board)

strong thread

picture frame

WORKING THE CROSS STITCH

Tack (baste) guidelines in both directions across the middle of the Hardanger. Work the cross stitch using three strands of cotton over two pairs of threads.

1 To make up: once complete, press on the reverse side. Stretch over the mount board (backing board) and fit into a frame of your choice.

DMC		
▶▶ 702	⁄⁄	444
◇◇ 970	◢◢	797
▨▨ 996	▬▬	310
� 666	⠿⠿	Blanc

Backstitch

—— 310

French knots

❤ 310 ——

☆ Middle point

PENCIL POT

*This little bird adds a touch of fun to a plain pencil pot, but could
also be made into a greetings card or miniature picture.*

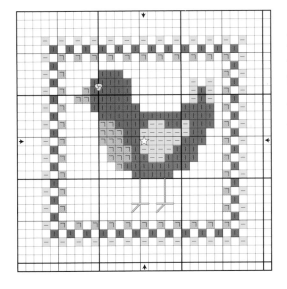

WORKING THE CROSS STITCH

Beginning with the border design,
work the cross stitch and the
backstitch using two strands of cotton
over two threads of linen. Once it is
complete, press on the reverse side and
finish with a French knot for the eye.

	DMC	Backstitch Anchor	French knots
冖冖	741		
– –	726	⎯ 741	☆ 726
■	917		☆ Middle point

YOU WILL NEED

*15 cm (6 in) square of white
28 count Irish linen*

*small embroidery frame
(flexihoop)*

*stranded cotton DMC
726, 741, 917*

tapestry needle

*10 cm (4 in) square of
burgundy fabric*

scissors

yellow pencil pot

double-sided tape

1 To make up: cut
the burgundy fabric
to fit the front of the box.
Stick in place with double-
sided tape. Cut the
embroidery slightly
smaller than the fabric and
stick in the middle to
finish.

CHILDREN'S BADGES

Children love badges to pin onto sweatshirts, hats and bags.
These designs are stitched on plastic canvas and are very easy to sew.

WORKING THE CROSS STITCH

All the designs can be worked on 10 or 14 count plastic canvas. The 10 count makes an 8 – 10 cm (3 – 4 in) badge and the 14 count makes one which measures 5 – 7 cm (2 – 2¾ in). Work the cross stitch motifs using two strands of Marlitt on 14 count plastic canvas or four strands on 10 count.

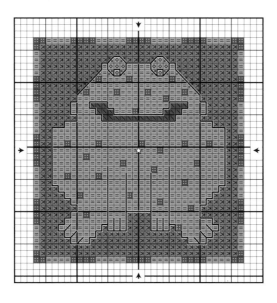

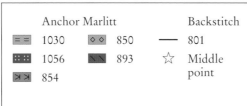

Anchor Marlitt			Backstitch
══ 1030	◇◆ 850		— 801
▦ 1056	◪ 893		☆ Middle point
▷▶ 854		

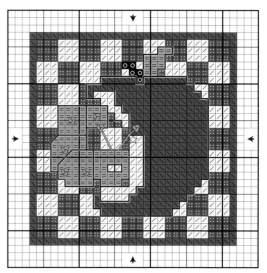

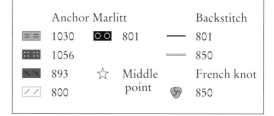

Anchor Marlitt		Backstitch
══ 1030	●● 801	— 801
▦ 1056		— 850
◪ 893	☆ Middle point	French knot
╱╱ 800		◕ 850

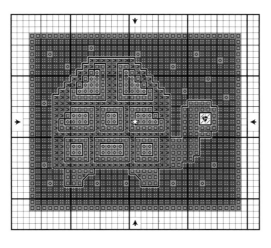

Anchor Marlitt		Backstitch
▦ 1056	╱╱ 800	— 801
▢▢ 814	
◇◆ 850	☆ Middle point	French knot
▷▶ 854		◔ 801

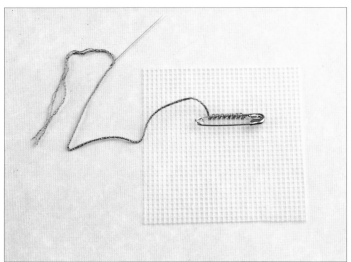

1 To make up: cut each badge out one hole away from the stitches. Cut a second piece of canvas the same size. Oversew a safety pin or brooch pin to the blank piece of canvas.

2 Hold the two pieces together and oversew, using two or four strands depending on the count of the canvas. Slip the ends between the layers and snip.

BATHROOM CABINET

This fun cabinet was handmade in pine and painted with red and white stripes to match the cross stitch design.

YOU WILL NEED

30 x 40 cm (12 x 16 in) blue 32 count linen

tacking (basting) thread

needle

embroidery hoop (frame)

stranded cotton DMC white, 310, 321, 322, 444, 824, 839, 948

tapestry needle

two pieces of mount board (backing board) each 28 x 38 cm (11 x 15 in)

craft knife

safety ruler

strong thread

panel pins

hammer

WORKING THE CROSS STITCH

Tack (baste) guidelines across the middle of the linen in both directions. Work the cross stitch using two strands of cotton but use only one strand for the backstitch. Press on the reverse side when complete.

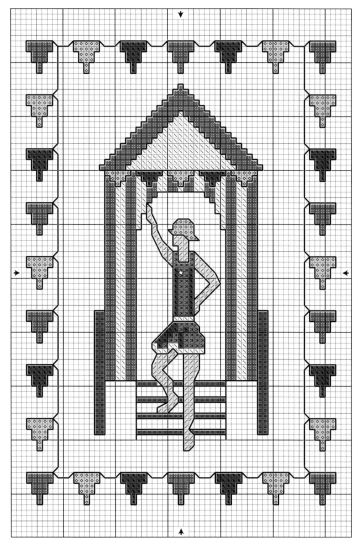

DMC		Backstitch	
839	824	— 310	
321	948		
322	white	☆ Middle point	
444			

1 To make up: cut the mount board (backing board) to fit into the opening in the door. Stretch the embroidery and fit into the door. Place a second piece of mount board behind the embroidery and fix in position using panel pins.

EMBROIDERED LINEN SHIRT

Decorate a plain shirt for a special occasion with this simple and elegant design in glistening embroidery threads.

YOU WILL NEED

plain linen shirt
Anchor Marlitt 864, 1003, 1036, 1040, 1140
tapestry needle
scissors

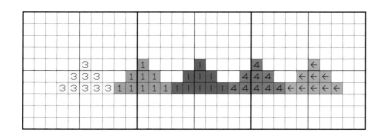

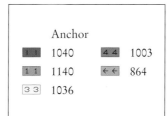

Anchor		
1 1 1040	4 4	1003
1 1 1140	← ←	864
3 3 1036		

WORKING THE CROSS STITCH

This shirt is made from fabric with quite a prominent, even weave which made it easy to work the cross stitch directly onto the fabric. If you want to work on a finely woven fabric use the waste canvas technique to keep the stitches even.

1 Choose a shirt with a long pointed collar which has the straight grain of the fabric following the outside edge of the collar. Starting 1 cm (3⁄8 in) in from the edge, work the cross stitch using two strands of cotton. Begin and finish the threads as neatly as possible on the reverse side.

2 Following the same sequence of colours, work a single cross stitch between the buttonholes on the front band of the shirt.

3 Finish the embroidery on the shirt by working the cross stitch design along the edge of the cuffs.

DECORATIVE BATH MAT

This plain cotton bath mat has been stitched with large swirls and cross stitches to co-ordinate with the bathroom accessories.

YOU WILL NEED

natural cotton bath mat

tacking (basting) thread

needle

soft cotton Anchor 11, 13, 228, 242, 305, 307

large sharp needle

scissors

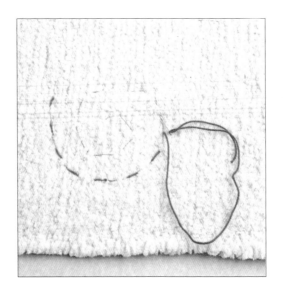

1 Stitching the lines about 2.5 cm (1 in) apart, tack (baste) twelve large swirls spaced evenly over the bath mat. Leave a 5 cm (2 in) end of soft cotton on the reverse side and stitch the spirals using 2.5 cm (1 in) running stitches. When you reach the end of the spiral, work back along the stitching line to fill in the spaces.

2 Work two spirals in each colour and then tie the ends of the cotton together with a secure knot.

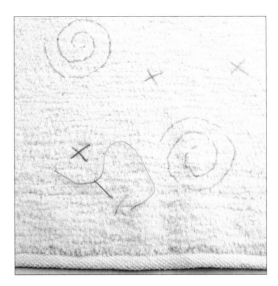

3 Work the cross stitches in between the spirals, beginning and finishing the thread in the same way. Finish the mat with a row of different coloured cross stitches along each end.

PLUM CURTAINS

Linen bands stitched with juicy plums add the finishing touch
to these large check cotton curtains.

YOU WILL NEED

8 cm (3 in) bleached linen band,
Inglestone Collection 980/80

scissors

tacking (basting) thread

needle

pins

stranded cotton Anchor 69, 70,
72, 212, 373, 905

tapestry needle

pair of green check curtains

sewing machine

sewing thread

WORKING THE CROSS STITCH

The amount of linen band required will depend on the width of the curtains. Cut a piece of linen about 10 cm (4 in) longer than the width of the curtains and fold in half crossways. Tack (baste) a guideline down the crease. Measure and mark with a pin every 20 – 25 cm (8 – 10 in) in both directions, keeping the last pins about 15 cm (6 in) from the end of the linen band, then tack guidelines in both directions. The positioning of the motifs will need adjusting depending on the width of your curtains.

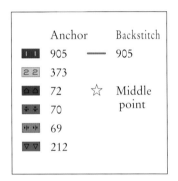

Anchor		Backstitch
1 1	905	⎯⎯ 905
2 2	373	
⬠⬠	72	☆ Middle point
✣✣	70	
❚❚	69	
▽▽	212	

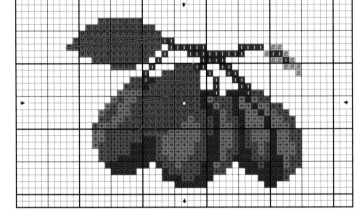

1 Work the plum motifs in the centre of the linen using two strands of cotton over two threads. Once complete, work the backstitch.

2 To make up: pin the linen band along the top of the curtain hem, taking the excess band onto the reverse side of the curtain. Turn under the raw edges and tack in position. Stitch along both sides close to the edge. Press on the reverse side and complete the second curtain to match.

PLUM BOX

This little painted box has an insert panel in the lid
which is ideal for a small piece of cross stitch.

WORKING THE CROSS STITCH

Work the cross stitch using a single strand of cotton over one thread of the linen. You will find it easier to work the plum first and then the background.

YOU WILL NEED

15 cm (6 in) square of white 28 count linen

small embroidery frame (flexihoop)

stranded cotton DMC 498, 581, 718, 732, 791, 814, 817, 905, 907, 936, 3721, 3731, 3746, 3810

tapestry needle

papier mâché box with insert, Decorative Arts

two shades of yellow acrylic paint

sponge

8 cm (3 in) square of wadding (batting)

8 cm (3 in) square of thin card (cardboard)

scissors

double-sided tape

1 To make up: sponge paint the box with the lighter paint and allow to dry. Sponge the second colour on top, allowing the light paint to show through.

2 Press the embroidery on the reverse side. Stretch the linen over the wadding (batting) and card, then fit inside the lid. Secure the insert panel using double-sided tape.

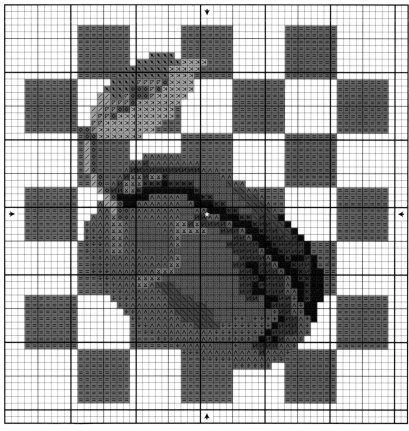

DMC					
═ ═	3810	▽ ▽	732	⋉ ⋉	814
⋮⋮⋮	718	╱ ╱	581	⋉ ⋉	3731
⊳ ⊳	907	⧄ ⧄	817	█ █	791
◇ ◇	936	⋈ ⋈	498	⋇ ⋇	3746
⋉ ⋉	905	∧ ∧	3721	☆	Middle point

CLOCK

Navy and cream paint has been cracked with crackle varnish to make
an unusual frame for this beautiful Assisi work.

YOU WILL NEED

20 cm (8 in) square of 18 count
navy Aida, Zweigart E3793

tacking (basting) thread

needle

Anchor stranded cotton 1223

tapestry needle

scissors

22 cm (9 in) square of
6 mm (¹/₄ in) thick MDF

hand drill with 10 mm (³/₈ in)
drill bit

1.2 m (1¹/₃ yd) wood architrave

hand saw

wood glue

masking tape

sandpaper

acrylic paint in dark blue and
cream

crackle varnish

paint brushes

clock mechanism with plastic
hands

14 cm (5¹/₂ in) square of
mount board (backing board)

pencil

strong thread

double-sided tape

WORKING THE CROSS STITCH

Tack (baste) guidelines across the middle of the Aida in both directions. Work the backstitch using a single strand of cotton. Fill in the background with rows of cross stitch. Press on the reverse side when complete.

Anchor	
==	1223
Backstitch	
—	1223
☆	Middle point

1 To make up: drill a 10 mm (³/₈ in) hole in the centre of the MDF. Mitre one end of the wood trim, measure 14 cm (5¹/₂ in) along the inside edge and mitre the other end. Saw another three pieces the same size. Spread glue on the underside and mitred edges of the wood trim and stick to the MDF. Tape the frame together and allow to dry, then sand the edges.

2 Paint the frame with dark blue paint. Let each layer dry before applying the next. Paint with a coat of crackle varnish, then with a coat of cream paint. The last coat can be dried with a hair dryer which will help the cracks to form. Trim the clock hands if necessary and paint in the same way.

3 Check that the mount board (backing board) fits inside the frame. Mark the position of the hole and cut one in the mount board. Stretch the embroidery over the board, mitring the corners neatly, and trim away any excess fabric. Cut into the fabric carefully and insert the front of the clock mechanism into the hole. Stick the mount board onto the frame and screw on the rest of the clock fitments.

YIANNI'S TAVERNA

This peaceful seaside scene was inspired by a typical Greek taverna and conjures up a summer holiday feeling.

YOU WILL NEED

45 x 50 cm (18 x 20 in) Antique white 28 count evenweave linen

tacking (basting) thread

needle

stranded cotton DMC white, 350, 400, 435, 437, 598, 646, 648, 712, 747, 842, 988, 3024, 3348

tapestry needle

21 x 23 cm (8¼ x 9 in) mount board (backing board)

strong thread

picture frame

WORKING THE CROSS STITCH

Tack (baste) guidelines across the middle of the linen in both directions and work the cross stitch using two strands of cotton. Press carefully on the reverse side when complete.

1 To make up: stretch the embroidery over the mount board (backing board) and fit into a suitable picture frame of your choice.

DMC	
==	350
⁞⁞	400
⤨⤨	435
◇◇	437
◥◥	598
▽▽	646
∕∕	648
╲╲	712
ИИ	747
∧∧	988
⋉⋉	3024
⤬⤬	3348
△△	white
÷÷	842

— Backstitch
646

☆ Middle point

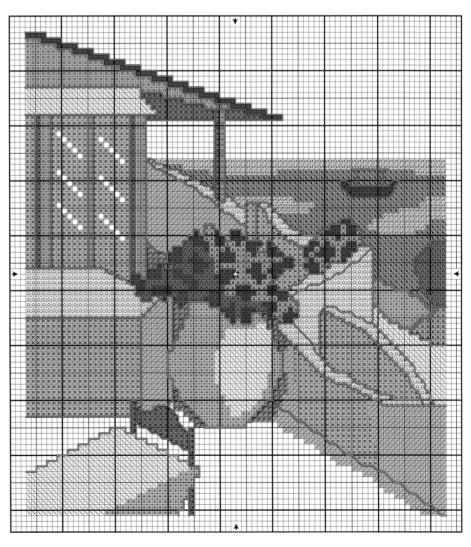

KEY HOLDER

Keys have a habit of being in the wrong place at the wrong time.
This cleverly designed key holder will ensure that you do not lose them.

WORKING THE CROSS STITCH

As the quantities used are small, don't feel that you need to buy every thread listed for this project. Use stranded cotton from your own collection to match the colours shown. Stitch the different doors onto the Aidaplus, keeping the threads as neat as possible on the reverse side.

1 To make up: paint the blank key holder with two coats of paint. Allow to dry and then fit the supplied hooks and hanging ring.

2 Cut out the completed designs close to the stitching. Aidaplus doesn't fray, but take care not to cut any threads. Arrange on the base and glue in position

YOU WILL NEED

blank key holder

terracotta paint, Colourman 106

paintbrush

sheet of platinum Aidaplus, Zweigart

stranded cotton DMC 300, 301, 310, 350, 356, 422, 433, 451, 500, 503, 611, 613, 677, 729, 740, 798, 817, 926, 927, 928, 932, 977, 986, 989, 3047, 3346, 3756, 3799, white

embroidery needle

scissors

all-purpose glue

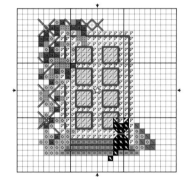

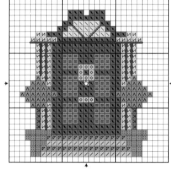

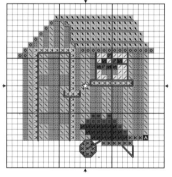

DMC		Backstitch
451	white	— 433
740	928	— 817
986	817	— 3799
989		☆ Middle point
310		

DMC		Backstitch
350	926	— 817
356	927	— 3799
433	928	
729	3047	☆ Middle point
817	3346	

DMC	817	Backstitch
300	928	— 611
301	977	— 3799
422	986	
611	3799	☆ Middle point
613	926	

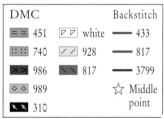

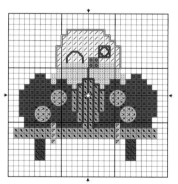

DMC	Backstitch	
611	— 611	☆ Middle point
613	— 310	
677		French knots
928		
932		611

DMC		Backstitch
500	927	— 503
503	3756	— 3799
729	3799	
798		☆ Middle point
926		

ROMAN BLIND

*This stunning blind is made all the more dramatic by the choice of
bold striped fabric shaded from dark to light blue.*

YOU WILL NEED

measuring tape

striped cotton fabric

*25 cm (10 in) wide 10 count
waste canvas*

tacking (basting) thread

needle

*stranded cotton DMC four
skeins of 700, two skeins of 307
and one skein each of 105, 743,
995 (approximate quantities)*

embroidery needle

pencil

ruler

binding tape

pins

sewing machine

sewing thread

scissors

*fusible bonding web to fit size
of blind*

brass rings

*2.5 x 5 cm (1 x 2 in) wood strip
the width of the window*

hand saw

tacks

hammer

screw eyes

fine non-stretch cord

*2.5 cm (1 in) wooden batten the
width of the window*

*cleat (for winding the cord
round)*

WORKING THE CROSS STITCH

Measure the height and width of your
window and add 8 cm (3 in) to the
width and 15 cm (6 in) to the length.
You will need two pieces of fabric this
size for the blind. Tack (baste) the
waste canvas 15 cm (6 in) from the
bottom of one piece of fabric. Mark

the centre and work the cross stitch
using three strands of cotton.
Continue the design out towards each
side, stopping after a complete tree.
Fray the canvas and pull out the
threads one at a time. Press on the
reverse side when complete.

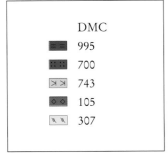

DMC	
══	995
┊┊┊	700
⟩⟩	743
◇◇	105
✗✗	307

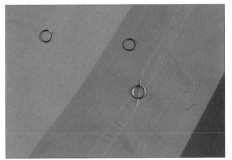

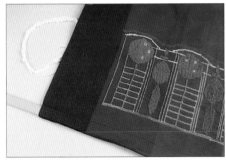

1 To make up: draw vertical lines down the right side of the lining fabric about 30 cm (12 in) apart with the outside lines about 8 cm (3 in) in from the edge. Pin and tack tape down all these lines and machine stitch down both sides. Iron fusible bonding web to the reverse side of the embroidered fabric. Remove the backing paper and lay the lining on top. Making sure the fabric is flat, press the layers together.

2 Turn in a 2.5 cm (1 in) hem down both sides of the blind and stitch. Turn up and stitch a 4 cm (1½ in) hem along the bottom edge. Making sure they are quite level, sew rings to the tapes every 15 cm (6 in) starting just above the hem.

3 Cut a headboard to fit the width of the window. Hammer in tacks to fix the top of the blind to the edge of the board. Fix screw eyes to the underside of the board so that they line up with the rings on the blind. The last ring on the right hand side should be large enough to take all the cords.

TO FINISH

Thread a length of cord through the large screw eye and down through the first line of rings. Knot it to the bottom ring. Thread cords through the other lines of rings in the same way, bring the cords together, and then tie a knot just below the large screw eye and plait the excess cord. Tie a knot at the end and trim. Slip the batten into the bottom hem and slip stitch both ends. Fit the heading board above the window and screw the cleat in at a comfortable height.

CHAMBRAY PILLOWCASE

Monograms give bed linen a touch of class. Choose your own initials to stitch in the corner of a classic Oxford pillowcase.

YOU WILL NEED

chambray Oxford pillowcase

small embroidery frame
(flexihoop)

10 cm (4 in) square of 10 count
waste canvas

stranded cotton Anchor 2

tacking (basting) thread

embroidery needle

white stranded cotton

Anchor	
■ ■	342

WORKING THE CROSS STITCH

Fit the embroidery hoop (frame) inside the pillow case and tack (baste) the canvas in the corner. Work the cross stitch design using three strands of cotton.

1 Once complete, fray and remove the canvas threads one at a time. Press on the reverse side. Stitch the same monogram on the corner of a matching sheet or duvet cover.

MINIATURE PICTURE

*These tiny frames are very popular and this design would make
a delightful gift for a partner or friend.*

WORKING THE CROSS STITCH

Fit the linen into the frame
(flexihoop) and work the cross
stitch border using a single strand
of cotton over two threads.
Complete the heart and work the
backstitch to finish the design
and press on the reverse side.

1 To make up: remove the back from the
frame and use the card insert to mount
the embroidery. Stick the wadding (batting) to
the card, trim the embroidery to an 8 cm (3 in)
square and stretch the fabric over the wadding,
sticking it down on the reverse side.

2 Fit the embroidery into the frame.
Add another layer of card (cardboard) if
required and fit the back.

YOU WILL NEED

*15 cm (6 in) square of
36 count linen*

*small embroidery frame
(flexihoop)*

*stranded cotton Anchor 133,
152, 226, 289*

tapestry needle

*ready-made frame with a 5 cm
(2 in) window*

*6 cm (2½ in) square of
wadding (batting)*

double-sided tape

scissors

Anchor		Backstitch	
5 5	289	——	226
7 7	152		
8 8	133	☆	Middle point
↑ ↑	226		

CAFETIERE COVER

*Keep fresh coffee warm with this stylish cover, designed to fit a
standard one-litre (two-pint) cafetière.*

YOU WILL NEED

*20 x 36 cm (8 x 14 in) white
14 count Aida*

tacking (basting) thread

needle

interlocking bar frame

*stranded cotton Anchor 148,
360, 370, 373, 398, 846*

tapestry needle

scissors

*30 cm (12 in) blue and white
patterned fabric*

*15 x 28 cm (6 x 11 in) wadding
(batting)*

pins

sewing machine

sewing thread

bodkin

WORKING THE CROSS STITCH

Tack (baste) guidelines across the
middle of the Aida in both directions
and work the cross stitch using two

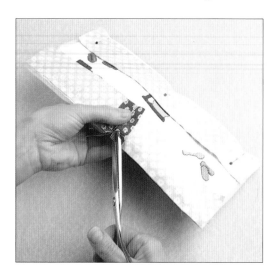

strands of cotton. Once complete,
work the backstitch and press the
embroidery on the reverse side.

1 To make up: cut the embroidered
panel and a piece of patterned fabric
the same size as the wadding (batting).
Tack the layers together with the wadding
in between the fabrics. Cut three 6 x 38 cm
(2½ x 15 in) strips of patterned fabric.
With right sides facing, pin one piece along
the bottom edge of the cover. Cut the other
two strips in half. Cut a "v" in the centre of
the top seam allowance. Fold over a 5 mm
(¼ in) turning at one end of two of the
short strips and butt the folds in the centre.
Pin and tack along the top edge, and stitch
using a 12 mm (½ in) seam allowance.

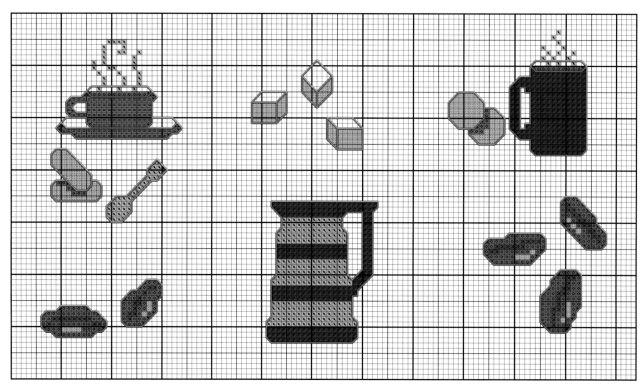

Anchor					Backstitch
▤	846	360	⊠	398	—— 360
⠿	373	370	▨	148	

2 Turn under 12 mm (½ in) and fold the bindings to the reverse side. Pin and tack in position. Snip the top fold of the binding and tuck the end inside. Slip stitch along each side of the "v" and along the edges of the binding.

3 Cut two bias strips of patterned fabric about 30 cm (12 in) long and make them into rouleaux. Tack one to the middle of each side with the long end facing onto the cover. Pin and tack (baste) the remaining binding strips to the sides. Stitch to the edge of the top and bottom bindings. Trim the ends, turn in and fold the binding to the reverse side. Slip stitch the binding to complete the cafetière cover.

SHELF BORDER

Stitch this smart teddy bear border, sewing a different coloured bow tie on each bear, and make a matching cushion.

YOU WILL NEED

10 cm (4 in) wide Aida band with red edges, Zweigart E7195

measuring tape

scissors

pins

tacking (basting) thread

needle

stranded cotton Anchor 369, 370, 403

for bow ties 4, 6; 38, 42; 108, 111; 217, 208; 293, 297

tapestry needle

sewing thread

double-sided tape or coloured drawing pins

WORKING THE CROSS STITCH

Measure the length of the shelf and cut a piece of Aida band the same length plus 5 cm (2 in) for turnings. Each bear is about 8 cm (3 in) wide. Decide on the spacing of the bears and mark the centre line of each with a pin. Tack (baste) guidelines across the band at each pin and again along the middle of the band to mark the centre of each bear. Work the cross stitch using two strands of cotton, changing the colours in the bow ties on each bear. Once complete, work the backstitch using two strands of cotton and press on the reverse side.

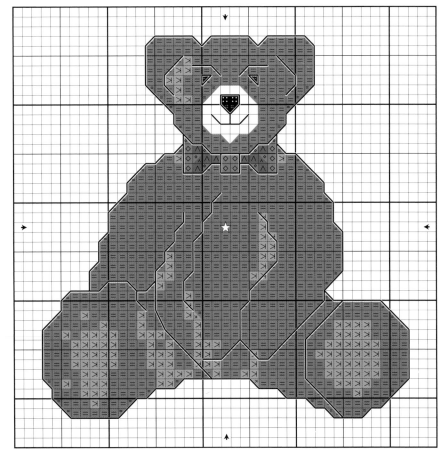

1 To make up: trim and turn under a narrow hem at each end of the band. You could either use coloured drawing pins or double-sided tape to fix the border in position on the shelf.

❖ ❖ ❖ ❖ ❖

NEEDLECRAFT TIP

To make a matching cushion panel, divide a 40 cm (16 in) square of 7 count canvas in four. Allowing a 5 cm (2 in) margin round the outside edge, cross stitch a bear in the middle of each square using tapestry wool, and fill in the background to match the decor of the room.

Anchor		Backstitch
▬▬ 370	◇◇ 38	— 403
▦▦ 403	^^ 42	
➤➤ 369		☆ Middle point

CHILD'S WAISTCOAT

Denim can be given a much softer appearance with the addition of some simple appliqué flowers and big bold cross stitches.

WORKING THE CROSS STITCH

Using the vanishing marker pen, measure and mark dots every 1.5 cm (⅝ in) round the front and bottom edges of the waistcoat. Sew large pink cross stitches using all six strands of cotton, slipping the needle between the layer of denim to get to the next mark. Sew two tiny back stitches on the reverse side to secure the thread, and trim neatly.

YOU WILL NEED

child's denim waistcoat
vanishing marker pen
ruler
stranded cotton Anchor 254, 894, 939
embroidery needle
scraps of cotton fabric
15 cm (6 in) square of fusible bonding web
scissors
four small 4-hole buttons

1 To make up: iron fusible bonding web onto the reverse side of the fabric scraps and cut out 16 petals. Remove the paper backing and iron the petals in position on the pockets and on the back of the waistcoat. Sew the petals in place with cross stitches.

2 Sew a button in the middle of each flower with blue stranded cotton. Sew a small green cross stitch in the corners of the top pocket and a row along the top of the lower pockets. Thread blue stranded cotton underneath the cross stitches on the pockets to finish.

CHILD'S BAG

This bag will appeal to all ages and will become a firm favourite with children and young teenagers to hold their bits and pieces.

YOU WILL NEED

28 x 100 cm (11 x 39 in) blue gingham

scissors

stranded cotton Anchor 225, 311, 894, 1028

embroidery needle

5 x 25 cm (2 x 10 in) pink denim

fusible bonding web

18 x 46 cm (7 x 18 in) blue denim

pins

sewing machine

sewing thread

tacking (basting) thread

1.5 cm (⁵⁄₈ in) button

WORKING THE CROSS STITCH

Cut a piece of gingham about 10 x 14 cm (4 x 5½ in) and press under a small 1 cm (³⁄₈ in) turning all round. Using three strands of cotton, sew the cross stitch border. Iron fusible bonding web onto the reverse side of a 5 cm (2 in) square of pink denim. Cut out three small hearts, remove the backing paper and iron onto the gingham. Sew in place with tiny stitches and stitch a blue cross in the middle of each heart to complete. Press on the reverse side.

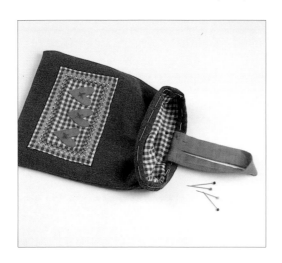

1 To make up: fold the blue denim in half crossways and open out. Pin the gingham patch on the top half and stitch. With the embroidery to the inside, fold the denim in half again and stitch both sides. Make a slightly narrower gingham lining in the same way and insert into the bag. Turn over a 2.5 cm (1 in) hem. With right sides facing, fold the pink denim strip in half lengthways and stitch the long edge. Trim and press the seam open, then turn through and press again with the seam at the centre back. Fold the strip to make a loop and pin under the hem at the centre back. Tack in position then stitch round the lower edge of the hem. Fold the loop back on itself and stitch.

2 Cut an 8 x 100 cm (3 x 39 in) strip of gingham and sew large cross stitches up the middle. Fold lengthways with the embroidery to the inside and stitch the long seam. Trim and press the seam open, then turn through and press again with the seam down the centre back. Turn under 12 mm (½ in) at each end of the strap and pin over the side seams. Tack (baste) and stitch securely. Sew the button on the front of the bag and sew a large cross stitch to hold the loop flat.

KITCHEN HANGING

*Kitchens are busy places and often neglected, but you could change
things by making this delightful decoration to hang on the wall.*

YOU WILL NEED

*15 x 30 cm (6 x 12 in) cream 28
count evenweave linen*

scissors

tacking (basting) thread

needle

interlocking bar frame

*stranded cotton DMC 312, 316,
435, 743, 3802, 3815, 3823*

tapestry needle

sewing machine

sewing thread

*two 11 cm (4⅜ in) squares of
wadding (batting)*

*5 cm (2 in) of 15 mm (⅝ in)
ribbon or tape*

pins

*40 cm (16 in) plant support or
46 cm (18 in) of wire with the
ends bent over*

bay leaves and dried apple slices

WORKING
THE CROSS STITCH

Cut the linen in half crossways.
Tack (baste) guidelines across
the middle of one piece in both
directions and work the cross
stitch using two strands of cotton
over two threads. Once complete,
work the backstitch using one
strand of cotton and then press
on the reverse side.

DMC		
═ ═ 3802	▽ ▽	3815
⫶⫶ 312	‖ ‖	3823
＞＞ 316		Backstitch
◇◇ 435	—	3823
⋈ ⋈ 743	☆	Middle point

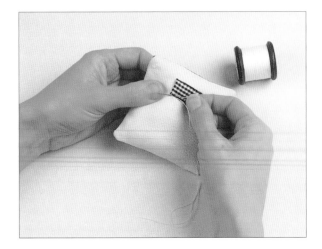

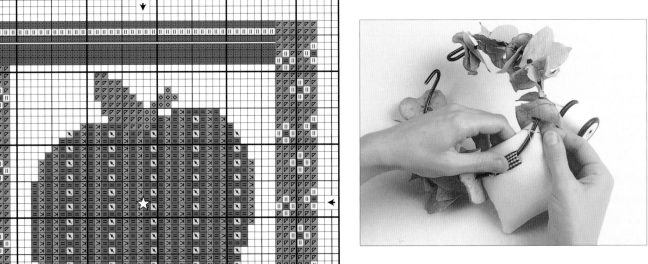

1 To make up: with the embroidery facing
in, sew the two pieces of linen together.
Stitch two threads away from the cross stitch
and leave a 5 cm (2 in) gap at the bottom. Trim
the seams and corners and turn through. Tuck
the wadding inside and slip stitch the gap. Fold
over the ends of the ribbon and pin to the back
of the cushion, 2 cm (¾ in) down from the top.
Oversew on both long sides.

2 Thread the cushion onto the wire loop.
Make small holes in the bay leaves and
thread onto the wire with slices of dried apple in
between. Some of the larger bay leaves are bent
over and threaded through again to create a
looser effect. Oversew the corners of the cushion
to hold them secure, loop over the ends of the
wire and hang in the kitchen.

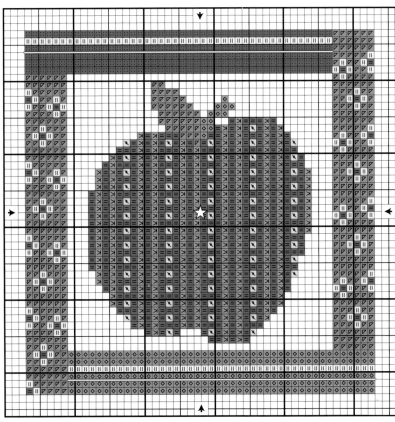

POT HOLDER

This colourful and stylish tile design was inspired by the lemon trees and deep blue sea of the Mediterranean.

YOU WILL NEED

15 cm (6 in) square of white 14 count Aida

tacking (basting) thread

needle

interlocking bar frame

stranded cotton DMC 307, 322, 336

tapestry needle

scissors

pins

two 23 cm (9 in) squares of dark blue chintz (glazed cotton)

sewing machine

sewing thread

10 cm (4 in) navy cord

10 cm (4 in) cushion pad

WORKING THE CROSS STITCH

Tack (baste) guidelines across the middle of the Aida in both directions and work the cross stitch using two strands of cotton. Press on the reverse side once complete.

1 To make up: trim the Aida to a 13 cm (5 in) square, mitre the corners and turn under 12 mm (½ in) on all sides. Pin, tack and stitch in the centre of one piece of chintz (glazed cotton). Fold the cord in half and sew it, loop facing in, to one of the corners.

DMC		
═ ═	307	☆ Middle point
∷∷	322	
➤ ➤	336	

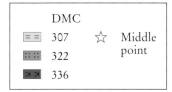

2 With right sides facing, sew the pieces of chintz together, with a gap on one side. Trim the seams and across the corners and turn through.

3 Insert the cushion pad and pin in the middle of the cover. Tack round the edges of the cushion pad and stitch. Slip stitch the gap closed to finish.

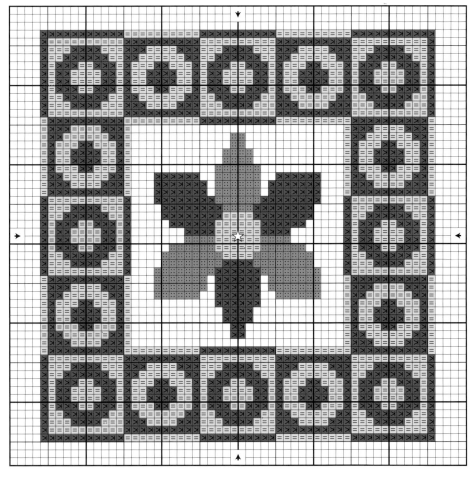

RUCKSACK

Rucksacks are extremely useful bags for all kinds of activities.
Sew the zebra panel to your own bag
or make this one following the easy instructions.

YOU WILL NEED

20 x 25 cm (8 x 10 in) white
18 count Aida

tacking (basting) thread

needle

interlocking bar frame

stranded cotton Anchor white,
22, 189, 297, 399, 403, 410

tapestry needle

paper

pencil

scissors

pins

1.50 m (1⅝ yd) of 115 cm
(45 in) wide berry canvas

sewing machine

sewing thread

four large "D" rings

10 large eyelets and tool

white cotton cord

button

14 x 18 cm (5½ x 7 in)
fusible bonding web

WORKING THE CROSS STITCH

Tack (baste) guidelines across the middle of the Aida in both directions and work the cross stitch border using two strands of cotton. Next, work the zebra design and press on the reverse side once complete.

1 To make up: enlarge the template and cut out the pattern. Pin the front and back panels together down both long sides and stitch. Press the seams flat and fold in half with the seams to the inside. Tack the raw edges together matching the seams. Top stitch round the folded edge and again 5 cm (2 in) away. Cut two 5 x 15 cm (2 x 6 in) pieces of canvas. Turn under 12 mm (½ in) on the long sides, fold in half and top stitch down both sides. Slide two "D" rings onto each strap, fold in half and pin, rings facing onto the bag.

2 Pin and tack the base to the bottom of the bag. Snip into the corners and stitch. Pin the flap pieces together and sew round the curved edge. Trim the seam and snip the curves. Turn through. Roll the seam between your fingers then press and top stitch. Cut two 5 x 60 cm (2 x 24 in) strips. Fold under a short end then make the straps as before. Pin and tack the raw edge between the seams and just below the second top stitching line. Pin the bag flap on top. Stitch across the flap, fold it over the raw edges and stitch a rectangle to secure.

3 Mark the position of the eyelets round the top of the rucksack and fit them following the manufacturer's directions. Thread a cord through the eyelets and tie 5 cm (2 in) from each end. Unravel the cord to make a tassel. Make a buttonhole on the bag flap and sew a button in place.

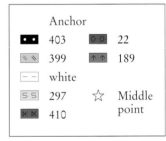

Anchor		
● ● 403	○ ○	22
◥ ◥ 399	↑ ↑	189
– – white		
⌐ ⌐ 297	☆	Middle point
✕ ✕ 410		

TO FINISH

Iron fusible bonding web onto the back of the cross stitch. Peel off the backing paper and pin the panel to the front of the bag. Press on the reverse side and back-stitch with 22 round the panel, one row out from the last stitching. Once the panel is complete, trim to about 1.5 cm (⅝ in) and fray the Aida.

BACKGROUND MOUNT

The exquisite embroidery makes a beautiful background for a small Christmas wreath which can be renewed each year.

YOU WILL NEED

30 cm (12 in) square of gold fleck 14 count Lurex Aida, Zweigart E3287

tacking (basting) thread

needle

embroidery hoop (frame)

fine gold braid Kreinik 221, 2122

stranded cotton Anchor 923

blending filament Kreinik 008

tapestry needle

2 m (2⅓ yd) of 3 mm (⅛ in) green ribbon

pins

Virginia creeper or clematis stems

wax gilt

small poppy heads, star anise and cupressus cones

all-purpose glue or glue gun

mount board (backing board)

strong thread

picture frame

WORKING
THE CROSS STITCH

Tack (baste) guidelines across the middle of the Aida in both directions. Work the cross stitch using the fine braid, as it comes, and two strands of cotton with the blending filament. Lay the ribbon diagonally across the embroidered panel. Pin and tack it securely in position at both ends, then sew an upright cross stitch with fine braid 221 where the ribbons overlap. Block the design when it is completed.

1 To make up: cut several fairly long lengths of creeper and coil them into a 15 cm (6 in) circle. Take another length of creeper and wrap this round and round the wreath to hold the coils together securely. Tuck the ends inside to complete the wreath.

	Balger Fine Braid
▬	221
⁞⁞	2122
▶▶	Balger Blending Filament 008 + Anchor 923

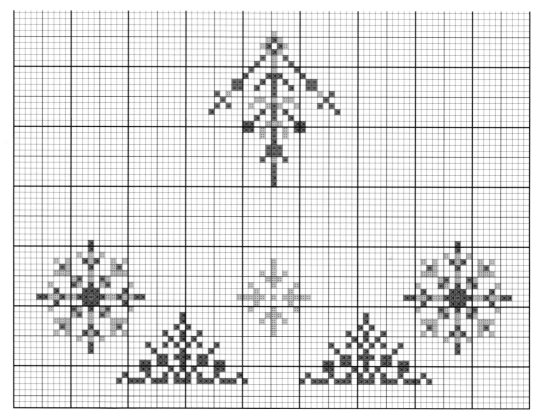

Stretch the embroidery over the mount board (backing board). Lay the wreath in position. Sew strong thread through the board in several places, taking it back through close to the original holes, and tie the ends securely. Fit into a frame of your choice.

2 Using your finger, wipe some wax gilt over the surface of the wreath. Once the wax gilt is dry it can be buffed gently with a soft cloth.

3 Arrange the dried plant material round the wreath until you are satisfied with the position, then glue. You can add more tendrils from the creeper, too. When the glue has dried, wipe more wax gilt over the plant material.

EGG CABINET

Eggs keep much better at room temperature than in the fridge.
This little cabinet with a broody hen on the front is ideal.

YOU WILL NEED

25 cm (10 in) square of pinky beige 28 count Jobelan

tacking (basting) thread

needle

embroidery hoop (frame)

wildflower cotton one skein each of terracotta/dark blue and spice

stranded cotton DMC white, 816, 841, 842, 3031

tapestry needle

egg cabinet with a 15 cm (6 in) door opening

paint, Colourman 104, 109, 114 (optional)

paintbrush

rubber gloves

medium steel wool

15 cm (6 in) square of mount board (backing board)

strong thread

15 cm (6 in) square of hardboard

panel pins

hammer

WORKING THE CROSS STITCH

Wildflower cotton is a variegated colour thread, not unlike flower thread or Nordin in weight and appearance. Open out the terracotta yarn and cut out the darkest blue sections. Work the main body of the hen in the variegated wildflower cotton and the shadows and head details in the blue.

Tack (baste) guidelines across the middle of the linen in both directions and work the cross stitch using one strand of wildflower cotton. Using two strands of stranded cotton, work the rest of the cross stitch. Once complete, work the backstitch and then press on the reverse side.

DMC	
– –	white
1 1	3031
2 2	841+842
3 3	841
H H	816
	Wildflower
	Terracotta/dark blue
✳ ✳	Spice
⊐ ⊐	Terracotta/dark blue (removed)
	Backstitch ~ DMC
—	841
☆	Middle point

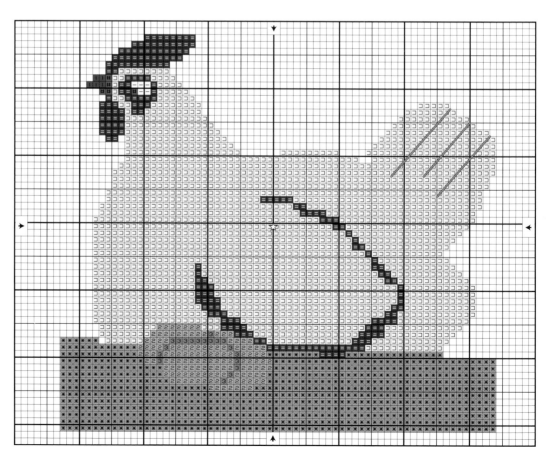

TO FINISH

Stretch the embroidery over the mount board (backing board) and fit inside the door frame. Fit a square of hardboard at the back and fix in place with panel pins.

1 To make up: paint the egg cabinet with blue paint and allow it to dry completely. Paint on top with the cream paint. You may need to add a touch of terracotta paint to tone the final look in with the linen.

2 Wearing rubber gloves to protect your hands, rub down the cabinet to reveal some of the blue paint and give the cabinet a "distressed" look. Brush out all the loose dust and wipe down with a barely damp cloth.

GIFT BAG

This luxurious bag with its hand-stitched monogram makes a very personal and beautiful wrapping for a special gift.

YOU WILL NEED

two 15 x 25 cm (6 x 10 in) pieces of metallic organza

sewing machine

sewing thread

two 15 x 25 cm (6 x 10 in) pieces of burgundy silk dupion (mid-weight silk)

scissors

pins

tacking (basting) thread

needle

5 cm (2 in) square of 14 count waste canvas

Anchor Marlitt 1034

stranded cotton Anchor 150

embroidery needle

46 cm (18 in) navy cord

bodkin

two navy tassels

1 To make up: fold over a 5 cm (2 in) hem on the short sides of the organza pieces and stitch down 4 cm (1½ in) on both sides. Repeat with the silk but turn up 1 cm (¼ in) of the hem before stitching. Trim across the corners, snip into the bottom of the stitching and turn through. With both hems facing the reverse side, layer the silk and organza together. Stitch across the hem twice, 1 cm (⅜ in) apart, to form a casing. Pin and tack (baste) the waste canvas in the bottom right corner, 6 cm (2⅜ in) from the raw edges.

2 Work the cross stitch using two strands of Marlitt and the backstitch using two strands of cotton. Once the embroidery is complete, remove the canvas threads one at a time. Press on the reverse side. Pin both sections together with right sides facing, and stitch round the three sides. Zigzag close to the stitching to neaten and trim the seam.

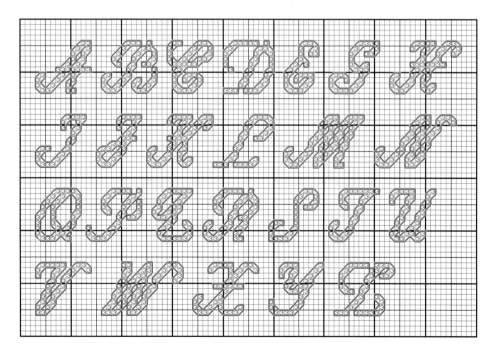

3 Turn the bag through and thread the cord through the casing with a bodkin. Slip one tassel over both cords to use as a fastening. Thread the other tassel onto one end of the cord. Overlap the ends of the cord and sew them together. Pull the cord gently until the join is inside the casing.

Anchor Marlitt	Backstitch ~ Anchor
3 3 1034	—— 150

TEMPLATES

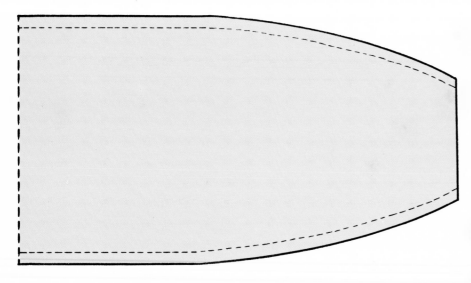

TIEBACKS

GARDEN APRON

EMBROIDERED BOOK

CHILD'S BAG

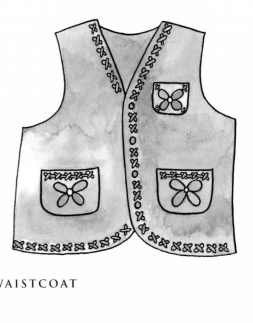

CHILD'S WAISTCOAT